DEDICATED TO MY BROTHER LAKAS SHIMIZU (2005-2013)

Foreword

By Bayan Shimizu

My name is Bayan Shimizu. I am thirteen years old and unlike others my age, I am grief-stricken. My beloved brother Lakas caught a common viral intestinal illness on Christmas 2013. I was 11. He was 8. My family and I didn't take it as dangerous, as the only apparent effects appeared to be stomachaches. I remember bringing him his Christmas presents.

Within 24 hours, the virus spread to his heart, abruptly ending his beautiful life. He died in my dad's arms, with my mom, grandpa and I flanking them. At the time, I had no idea that he died, and thought he only passed out. Within a few minutes, my cousins, aunts and uncles came, and my whole family thought he was only in a coma. We all rushed to a hospital emergency room, where my mom was called in to go see him. I anxiously waited to hear the news, hopefully that he was still alive. When I saw my mom return, I saw her face and knew the answer, but needed to ask. I couldn't accept it.

Recently, I realized Lakas actually died at that moment, when I thought he passed out in my dad's arms. The same grief I felt then came back now, as when his death was still fresh in my mind. The day after his death, I woke up to the question: do I consider myself an only child? I could not answer that question until weeks later.

I remain the sibling of Lakas and the son of Dan and Celine. I am the lover of just-being-alive-in-the-sense-of-not-being-dead. Devoted to the caring embrace of my family, whether in our quiet home or while traveling to new places, or the arms-in-the-air elation of victory while gaming with friends, I feel an overwhelming sadness from mourning my brother's death. While I feel bursts of happiness from completing seemingly impossible feats, the uncontrollable grief in the face of loss is always with me.

After Lakas died, nothing has been the same. Even going to school isn't simple. Nothing feels easy anymore. I know I am missing something, my constant companionship with my brother Lakas. I see his empty bed every morning, every night. But I need his bed here in our room because to get rid of it, is to take the first step in forgetting him. I don't think forgetting is inevitable. What I fear is the inevitability of death and the power of illness to take a robust life.

I consider the playful gift of puns as the raw expression of love in remembering my brother Lakas. I can see his exact face and his body in an explosion of laughter when hearing the perfect pun. I believe my writing puns expand my mind, and express my emotions. I also achieve fulfillment through establishing a hard work ethic. The power of creativity also builds long lasting bonds and special memories. It also gives me a sense of my possible future, for someday, I would like to be a prolific and productive author.

After publishing my first book, PUNISHMENT (2014), I realized how much puns could bring people together. My younger brother's close friends started to tell me many puns that they thought of, and kids in my neighborhood were telling me puns too. One particular thing is very important to me: that other kids who have lost siblings know that our lives are not over. You can produce and create things that will honor your lost loved ones, help shape your future and deepen your friendships.

When I see my brother Lakas' friends, and talk about how to make puns in our old school, where Lakas is supposed to be in the fourth grade, I can imagine him laughing at my puns, and trying to make his own. He would love being in this pun community. I love this very much. It makes me happy that Lakas and I may be remembered because of my books. In this, I am creating a new kind of inevitability. My life will be flavored with art, creativity, and community.

I would like to thank my family, especially my Mom and Dad for encouraging me to write and helping me to publish my books. Thanks to my godbrother Andrew James Ferrara-Jones, for creating and sharing with me a pun that became the beautiful title of this book. AJ wrote the pun in response to my first book PUNISHMENT. He sent me a video of himself, saying his puns were 'bad' and as he ripped a piece of paper labeled PUNS in half, he spoke the punch line: "they're tear-able!" This is now one of my favorite puns.

Amy Lin deserves many thanks for creating the illustrations that are held within this book. They are of my brother Lakas whom she knows very well since she drew pictures of him ever since he was in Kindergarten. Thank you for remembering my brother Lakas and animating his energy. I love seeing my brother's expressions and happiness in the images. My friend Pauline Vo designed the covers of both my books. I love her design that shows the playfulness of my puns and Mrs. Lin's art. Pauline is so creative in asking me for my favorite homophones for the cover.

My Auntie Maya Soetoro-Ng wrote a blurb for my first book and this book. When I visited her, she asked me about how I am living with the death of my brother, and I talked with her for an hour about how I felt. She is a really kind person and I feel very grateful she read my book. I am honored by Uncle Viet Nguyen's review of my book. It is very funny and smart.

I would like to thank many people at my school and in my community who read and bought my book. I especially appreciate my teachers, for educating me. Not just my English teachers, but also many other teachers really inspired me. You can see from my puns that I love Science, Social Sciences and History and I even have some Math problems, I mean, Math puns in my book.

Lastly, thanks to all the people who help me with my grief work. I refer to the multiple grief organizations like KARA and Camp Erin, my counselors, and my sibling loss group at Sutter Bereavement. If my brother Lakas were alive, I would never know these compassionate people who have helped me through my treacherous journey of grieving. I would rather Lakas were alive than to know these wonderful people. I recognize that Lakas is no longer physically present so I know I need their help to make it through. And I am also devoted to helping these organizations with my own volunteering and charity work. Part of the proceeds of my book will go to the Lakas Shimizu Philanthropy Fund, which helps other kids.

In this book, I honor my brother's life. You can see my love for him in these pages. Lakas is always with me. He will always be my brother no matter what.

After reading all that (like you should have), now let's move <u>foreword</u> in the book.

PUN I heard about some bunnies fighting. It was a hair-raising tale.

PUN I have lots of flare for calling for help.

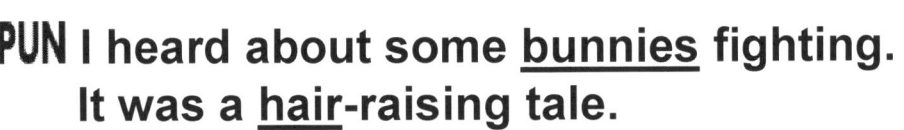

PUN <u>Stones</u> are great. They <u>rock</u>.

PUN When I saw <u>Smokey</u>*, I couldn't <u>bear</u> to start a fire.
   *The forest fire bear guy.

PUN Did you hear how they stopped that <u>huge animal</u>? They used a <u>BEARicade</u>.

PUN I don't like <u>vacuums</u>. They <u>suck</u>.

PUN A puzzle <u>angered</u> me, but after a while I was at <u>piece</u>.

PUN I had a bet to hit a <u>rooster</u>, but I <u>chickened</u> out.

PUN My first experience with <u>glue</u> really <u>stuck</u> with me.

PUN When flying in an empty <u>NASA rocket</u>, I realized there was too much <u>space</u>.

PUN A tyrant can never <u>measure up</u> to a good <u>ruler</u>.

PUN While talking about <u>trains</u>, the talk suddenly was about dogs. The conversation was really <u>derailed</u>.

PUN After seeing somebody rob an <u>adhesive</u> store, I was happy I had it all on <u>tape</u>.

PUN I really get a <u>kick</u> out of <u>soccer</u>.

PUN After somebody told me to try to make a <u>syringe</u>, I thought I'd take a <u>shot</u> at it.

PUN I was wondering if my <u>club</u> would knock me out, and then <u>it hit me</u>.

PUN When I left school, I was happy to be <u>divided</u> from <u>division</u>.

PUN When I was asked what was my favorite part of the <u>solar system</u>, I said "The sun. It's the <u>star</u> of the galaxy."

PUN If you get angry while playing <u>golf</u>, you've got to <u>putt</u> yourself together.

PUN I saw a <u>square</u> cut in half. It looked very out of <u>shape</u>.

PUN Many people complained about the high-priced <u>toll</u>, "It's not <u>fare</u>!"

PUN The <u>North Star isn't the brightest star</u>? You can't be <u>Sirius</u>*!
*the brightest star

PUN On TV, having somebody ignore <u>rare minerals</u> is comedy <u>gold</u>.

PUN Dogs are like <u>trees</u>. Their <u>bark</u> is worse than their bite.

PUN How nice <u>the wind</u> is really blows me <u>away</u>.

PUN At first I liked keeping <u>doors closed</u>, but then I <u>opened</u> up to them.

PUN Money from farming <u>apples</u> is a <u>fruit</u> of labor.

PUN It is very easy to <u>mess</u> around with a <u>mop</u>.

PUN Taking a picture of a <u>cage</u> really <u>captures</u> the moment.

PUN An email's least favorite food is spam.

PUN I have using a hammer nailed down.

PUN It's hard to be a <u>dog</u>. It's really <u>ruff</u>.

PUN When watching an <u>animal documentary</u>, I had to <u>paws</u> it many times.

PUN Entrances to <u>sewers</u> are <u>grate</u>.

PUN Cheddar puns are so <u>cheesy</u>.

PUN <u>Art</u> really <u>draws</u> my attention.

PUN To make <u>text bigger</u> is very <u>bold</u>.

PUN Why do kids play <u>soccer</u>? I don't <u>C.Y.</u>*

*A junior soccer league in California.

PUN Somebody asked if I was hungry for <u>numbers</u>. I said I already <u>8</u>.

PUN When a company found out the <u>phones</u> they made don't work, they had to <u>call off</u> the product.

PUN During a <u>play about metals</u>, iron always <u>steels</u> the show.

PUN Asking for <u>change</u> after making a purchase just makes <u>cents</u>.

PUN I like <u>rivers</u> better than lakes. Rivers have more <u>flow</u> in their movement.

PUN After my friend stole my <u>ice cream</u>, I felt <u>deserted</u>.

PUN <u>Pillows</u> are nice. They're always <u>soft</u> to you.

PUN I can always <u>count</u> on a <u>mathematician</u>.

PUN If you're a school <u>pencil</u>, you really need to stay <u>sharp</u>.

PUN When researching layers of <u>ground</u>, I always kept <u>digging</u> deeper.

PUN When multiple links make a <u>bracelet</u>, they have to <u>band</u> together.

PUN Some people decided to destroy a **landfill**. It was all a **waste**.

PUN A **transparent** person doesn't lie well. You can **see right through** him.

PUN These days, people who make <u>bombs</u> are rich. Their business is <u>booming</u>.

PUN I find <u>subtraction</u> much too <u>negative</u>.

PUN Caffeine with a <u>sore throat</u> is very <u>coughy</u>. (Coffee)

PUN You may think <u>lamps</u> are heavy, but they're actually very <u>light</u>.

PUN If you feel physically <u>sensitive</u> after not winning, you might be a <u>sore</u> loser.

PUN When <u>construction workers</u> are sad, you need to have them <u>build</u> up some happiness.

PUN The carpenter making <u>steps</u> was always <u>stairing</u>.

PUN It's a good <u>call</u> to buy a <u>phone</u>.

PUN Somebody told me they were going to dig a <u>mine</u>. The moment they hit it, it <u>exploded</u>.

PUN Some say <u>footwear</u> companies are corrupt, but you need to look at it from their <u>shoes</u>.

PUN A couple was supposed to come to a <u>Science</u> class, but they broke up - they didn't have <u>chemistry</u> anymore.

PUN Even though there was a huge <u>buildup</u>, the <u>construction of a building</u> was cancelled.

PUN These days at farms, you can find a <u>labyrinth</u> of crops. It's a corn <u>maize</u>.

PUN Dishonest <u>harps</u> are total <u>lyres</u>.

PUN Working for <u>7 days</u> can make somebody <u>week</u>.

PUN I'm <u>tolled</u> crossing the <u>bridge</u> costs $20.

PUN Did you hear about the underground <u>fruit</u> tree? It was <u>berry-d</u>.

PUN While <u>listening to farm animals</u>, I <u>herd</u> some cows.

PUN There were some birds lying near a pond. They were sitting ducks for hunters.

PUN Squids are incredible.

PUN I'm <u>threw</u> with <u>tossing</u> stuff!

PUN I met somebody who was scared of <u>Santa</u> and small spaces. They were <u>Claus</u>-trophobic!

PUN A stuffy <u>nose</u> is nothing to <u>sneeze</u> at.

PUN Touching <u>poison oak</u> is a <u>rash</u> decision.

PUN I feel like a <u>cube</u>. I have writer's <u>block</u>.

PUN <u>Golfing</u> is my cup of <u>tee</u>.

PUN There are so many puns about
    bombs, it makes me want to explode.

PUN Standing doesn't really sit with me.

PUN I've recently been <u>looking</u> into <u>glasses</u>.

PUN People in <u>graves</u> are always <u>coughin'</u>!

PUN Whenever I see <u>dirt</u>, it is <u>ground</u> up.

PUN I'd say **knitting** is **sew-sew**.

PUN When people told me about **round** swords, I didn't get the **point**.

PUN <u>Dogs</u> are smart. If you ask them what's on a <u>tree</u>, they say <u>bark</u>.

PUN Also, if you're <u>inside</u>, if you ask a <u>dog</u> what's above them, they say <u>roof</u>!

PUN If you ask a <u>dog</u> what <u>sandpaper</u> feels like, they say <u>ruff</u>!

PUN Going <u>left</u> is never <u>right</u>.

PUN While making <u>knots</u>, I feel all <u>tied</u> up.

PUN I met a robot with a <u>dent</u>. He felt really <u>bent</u> out of shape.

PUN After selling one million <u>tires</u>, I felt on a <u>roll</u>.

PUN My friend asked me what kind of <u>ship</u> he should get. I told him whatever <u>floats your boat</u>.

PUN Did you hear about that <u>imported fruit</u>? It was really <u>fresh</u> off the boat.

PUN Open <u>markets</u> are very <u>bazaar</u>.

PUN A truck barely made its last cargo drop off. It was a load off for the driver.

PUN You need to have drive to make cars.

PUN **Saying** something in your head is not **aloud**.

PUN After math class, I looked at **geometry** from a different **angle**.

PUN I met somebody who lived in a pile of <u>trash</u>. It was a total <u>dump</u>.

About the Author:
Bayan Shimizu is 13 years old. This is his second book.

About the Publisher:
Soken Studios produces books, video games, apps, and other projects.

Copyright Bayan Shimizu 2015.

All rights reserved. No part of this book may be reproduced or transmitted in any form without the express written consent of the author.

Published in the United States by Soken Studios.
www.sokenstudios.com

ISBN 978-1518871009

Illustrations by Amy Lin.

Book Cover Design by Pauline Vo.

Made in the USA
Middletown, DE
30 June 2024

56547594R00038